Within Within

For Lorna Crozier —
w/ gratitude
for your gifts —
your poetry and vision —

Within Within

Peter Levitt

Peter Levitt

Black Moss Press 2008

© Peter Levitt 2008

Library and Archives Canada Cataloguing in Publication

Levitt, Peter, 1946-

    Within Within / Peter Levitt.

Poems.

ISBN 978-0-88753-446-1

    I. Title.

PS3562.E949W58 2008   811'.54   C2008-902078-2

Cover image: Marty Gervais

Cover design: Mandy Boreski

Published by Black Moss Press, 2450 Byng Road, Windsor, Ontario N8W 3E8. Black Moss Press books are distributed by LitDistco. All orders should be directed there.

Black Moss acknowledges the generous support for its publishing program from The Canada Council for the Arts and The Ontario Arts Council.

The Canada Council | Le Conseil des Arts
for the Arts | du Canada

ONTARIO ARTS COUNCIL
CONSEIL DES ARTS DE L'ONTARIO

Other Books by Peter Levitt

Winter Still
*Fingerpainting on the Moon: Writing and Creativity
  as a Path to Freedom*
One Hundred Butterflies
Bright Root, Dark Root
Homage: Leda as Virgin
A Book of Light
Running Grass (Poems 1970 – 1977) Foreword by
  Robert Creeley
Two Bodies, Dark/Velvet
Poems

Books Translated by Peter Levitt

*A Flock of Fools: Ancient Buddhist Tales of Wisdom
  and Laughter* (Translated and Retold with Kazuaki
  Tanahashi)
Sky Stones by Pablo Neruda

Books Edited with Foreword by Peter Levitt

The Heart of Understanding by Thich Nhat Hanh
No Beginning, No End: The Intimate Heart of Zen
  by Jakusho Kwong

for Shirley

Acknowledgements

Grateful acknowledgement to the editors of the Windsor Review, and to (m)Öthêr Tøñgué Presš for the initial publication of some of these poems in the chapbook, *Winter Still*. I also thank the Canada Council for the Arts for their kind support during the writing of this manuscript.

My deepest thanks to Don Domanski and Robert Hilles for their insight, support and friendship during the period when this book was written. And, of course, my love and gratitude to my wife, Shirley Graham, for all she gives.

Black Moss Press would like to thank the talented team involved in the production of this book. Their labour has been invaluable in every respect. These include: Emily Beaton, Mandy Boreskie, Anne-Marie Charron, Bill Delisle, Kate Hargreaves, Lindsey Hindi, Donna Luangmany, Neda Marin, Janine Morris, Cristina Naccarato, Danielle Romanello, Melissa Schnarr-Rice, and Katie West.

Table of Contents

Pale Shadow

I rise early and walk to where light
enters the forest in silence

tentative as a new lover, my hands
leading me branch by branch

on the uneven path. Overhead,
the powerful stroke of wings

through air causes me to stop.
A sound like feathered oars

as the morning hunt begins,
I can just make out the direction

before the soft whirring disappears.
Two summers past my wife

looked on as an eagle dove
without warning into a flock

of ducks floating lazily near the marsh
at Cusheon Lake. The force of

the attack plunged the predator
beneath the surface as she watched

from shore. Then the eagle lifted its huge
form above the water, shook and tried

to rise, its claws clutching prey.
"There was no way it could

lift off," she told me. "The killer
and killed had become one body

and the weight wed them where they were."
Finally the eagle began to row,

he arched his great wings forward
into the lake and pulled against

death's enormous weight
until he reached the shallows

where water lilies tangle among fallen limbs.
Then he dragged his prey into the soft grass

to hide among the reeds,
his shadow on the water the last

thing my wife could see. There
is a silence that surrounds

this world of shadow and light,
an unmoving invisibility that clarifies

each thing as it is beside the next,
a membrane that shapes the detail,

one by one. It is how it all conjoins.
I walk in the woods beside

the river that rolls its soft tongue
among stones night and day.

It is not words that guide me,
not life or death or change or anything

I can name. It is the stillness before any
name is given and the stillness just after,

the unseen body that lives in the space
between trees, or flows beneath the earth's

green water. I hold the image of the eagle's
kill no different from the first time I saw

my children bathed in the birthing
blood that helped to keep them

alive. All words, all that die
or kill and struggle to survive

are pale shadows, transparencies
that return to their source at such a time,

the unmoving ground beneath the ground
where we stagger, or stride.

The Lens

Even removing the goat skin
gloves and rubbing his hands
does not bring warmth.
Not this morning. Subzero,
the thermometer says, and
he believes it as he gathers
wood from the shed before
the family starts to rouse.
Something is changing,
not just the hardening sky
as the invisible mill turns
white petals through the air.
He looks at the lake's slow freeze,
how long it took for the water
to solidify before the milky surface
arrived, and notices he slightly
cocks his head to see it.

He does not look in the old
way at anything anymore.
When did it begin? A lens,
thinner than the skin of ice
on winter berries has placed
itself in the corner of his eye.
It is through this transparency
he has begun to see the world.
It isn't just the lake.

Everything now passes through
this miniscule cataract in reverse,
this hole of clarity and reflection.

The rest of his eye still functions
as it always has. The black pupil
widens and shrinks as it was made to
with the coming and going of the light.
The green iris brightens, almost boasting
its unseasonable colour, and the sclera
is moist, brilliantly white and clear.
But the lens, wholly invisible to himself
and others, is what he goes to now,
to see the inside of what he looks at,
to sense how much of its time remains,
to touch its transience and even feel
its dying breath before it does,
though there is no sorrow in him,
or no extra sorrow, each thing felt
as tender and given a love it deserves.

"I have a new lover," he jokes
with his wife. "A new way to love."
He tries it out and finds it is faithful,
always there, which deepens his feeling.
Something he can count on in the midst
of so much else that is changing
to make his loneliness almost disappear.
The children he's had show themselves

one by one, the girl wearing a red jumper,
a Christmas dress, and smiling
with a front tooth gone, the boy
just big enough for his new bike,
tentative, bright eyed, wanting to please.
His parents too are there as he loads
his arms with aged alder and fir
to carry back to the house. It is almost
like cradling their bodies against his chest,
though he walks with the weight of knowing
they've already grown small in their graves
as his boots crunch along the path.

A good fire these logs need,
he tells himself. A good fire
they will make. And time,
time to go down slowly
even as the smoke makes
ghosts that dance and disappear
above the flue in the throat of stones.
The kind of time his wife
gives her figures in the kiln,
watched with an eye
keen to their needs, their baking,
to the changing of the glaze.

A Translation in Winter

1.

At noon the air grows cold,
the morning rain slows
to the pace of a lighter snow
and the fire in the stove
gives rise to the bright
face of a childhood friend
that presses from outside
against the window until
suddenly it grows clear.
Perfect, with still an unworldly
smile he remains unmarked
by what he never could have
guessed – certainly not his war.

It is not easy to hold back
what's known once a thing
has risen into the world,
it can weigh each day a little longer,
a little more until it is hard
in the morning to stand fully tall,
but for now the burst of snow
brightens the cold, blue air
and I hold only the joy
that such a face may still appear.

2.

My wife dreamed the face of our son
two years before he finally came,
and it was four more before she looked
across the room as he played in the quiet
concentration that illuminates a child:
"That's the face of the boy I saw in my dream.
Do you remember?"
To remember a dream –
I had to laugh:
"Is there anything else to recall?"

3.

I reach for the phone because
the worried love in my mother's
face calls as it used to do. Or
my father's deep voice saying
the syllables of my name –
to hear it once more.
A losing game now that they're gone.
A burial of all that's lost to everyone
in a place we commonly share.
Alone, I put the receiver down
and walk back across the room.
Silent, accepting, transient as a winter
storm, the trace of my steps
slowly disappears.

4.

Let it rain, then, or snow.
Let it all come down.
A world of light and shadow
is what we live in
and sometimes understand.
I rise in the morning from the dark
forms of this poem to find the brilliance
of a frozen field out my door
and the snow that lay its body
all night over the surface of the lake
while I slept lost and warm
beside the quiet breathing of my wife.

A cormorant that seems off course
arrives with the rising light,
lets out a cry and just now
lands on a spur of the fallen tree
that spans sixty feet from shore.
He scans the beauty of forbidding ice.
In summer my wife and son and I
swim out to this jumping log
and slither across its thick trunk
to leap and leap again into
our brief reflection and joy.

I've seen this bird in winter before.
He comes and goes in a time
not entirely his own. He flies
a life whose path is mystery
to me, except that he returns
these three or four years to
settle himself, to stand on
that very spot without moving,
wings spread out to dry.

Enough, then.
A bird flies like a bird
I tell myself again,
water is still, all the way down.

Frozen House

for Spalding

Light begins to return, though
the lake remains locked in ice.
No heat penetrates the solid ground.

One year ago a friend slipped
to the ferry stern as rehearsed,
then slid beneath the wake
until his lungs filled with the final
cold he had only imagined.

No note. No sign. No one certain
until spring when his body floated up
with others who submerged
in winter's despair. One by one
they rose from the thawing bed
like twisted flowers, their skin peeled,
petalled around white bone stems.
Then we knew.

That a man no longer –
That a soul could not –
That his sons might always –

It is sometimes hard each day
to breathe and move among the living
things of the world we've loved.

21

Winter stillness, the calling beauty
of its dark, grows so slowly upon the land,
we hardly notice until all the internal
sheaves of ourselves believe
in their frozen solitude,
the solidities of their isolate lives.

For years my mother sat beside her window
unmoving despite my call. Only
the fiercest love forced her eyes
to unblear, focus, and return. So many
ghosts waited beyond the cold glass.

Her sister and the baby dead in childbirth –
Her brother at seventeen mad as Mona Lisa –
Her mother hysterical in the streets –
The immigrant poverty of that –

Nothing beyond my window moves,
nothing above or below the ice
that can be seen. Even the sun
appears trapped, an outsider
pressing its face against
the sky's transparency.

Awake again all night long,
I stroke my ribs, the small
muscles between them that strap
me to their cage, and wonder

what future lies concealed
beneath the broken ground,
and how the body can bring itself
to rise against pain that seems
without beginning, that
even death may never end.

Within Within

Spring is within a plum twig, bearing the snow—cold
—Eihei Dogen, 1243

No one can say what this life is.
Snow, spring, plum twig and bearing,
each thing is cold cold cold
and cold cold cold
is snow, spring, plum twig and bearing.

This is within and this is
what is within. Bearing
sorrow in silence
or holding our happiness
for the world
are just plum twigs
bearing snow.

Shouting joy at passing cars
or whispering I'm going
to kill myself
is the heat of petals
in winter, the blossoming
of snow drops in spring.

Don't try and don't quit,
that's the best I can say.
People who love you

and people who need you
and people you love
and those you hate
come to the same thing.
No matter how you turn,
you can never turn fast
or far enough. There
is no escaping
the ten directions
or ten thousand things,
even when you die.

So take it easy.
Have a Cuban cigar.
Your shoulders are
wide as the path
is wide, your heart as open
as one blossom
two snow falls
three bows to the east
and four kisses,
one on each cheek.

Zuchinni and Peach

A beautiful and well-shaped imported peach ripens
on the back of an enormous zucchini. The event
takes place in my kitchen greenhouse window
which faces south and draws all the heat and light
the peach will require since it is early October and
we live in the northern world. I placed the peach
atop the zucchini toward the rear after giving it
a little squeeze and deciding it needed another
day. And, who knows, tomorrow it may be the
same. A little squeeze, another day. The peach
has an enviable life and since I will eat it when the
squeeze says *now* so that a bit of sweet will enter
me and become a seed of my own future, I am
happy. Across the lake the maple and alder leaves
turn yellow and red the exact colour of this peach,
and I can't believe how sometimes lucky the world
can feel.

At a poetry reading tonight the poet who knows
nothing of the secret ripening in my window
announces that the couplets she will read have
nothing to do with one another. She tells us this is
an ancient form. Any connections we make are the
result of our own imaginations leaping. I think of
them as small groups of acrobats practicing for the
evening performance in one of the three rings under
the Big Top, and I think of Frank O'Hara's prophetic

line that the slightest loss of attention leads to death.
Poetry. Love. The rest of living: If in the middle of a
trick just one couplet looks over at the one beside it,
it's all over. But does this mean that the poet is right
and they have nothing to do with one another, or
is it the opposite as words and bodies detach at the
stem and fly through the air?

It is an ancient form that the killing doesn't stop.
Children with faces reduced to a smudge stare
through the broken glass, wait for the heavy step,
watch as their fathers are taken away in chains or
shot in the yard or their mothers are dragged into
the back room of their shack by soldiers who shout
and laugh and either kick the door shut behind or
don't. An ancient form. Born young into a world
already old, Zukofsky said, and who in Byalistok,
Rwanda, Los Angeles, Sudan, Srebrenica would
deny him? The red cheeks at the window ripen
with shame, with fear, with the fertile blood seed
of a future killing they don't yet know but can feel
behind their eyes. When the conditions are right,
the cycle of murder and the cycle of nature ripen
the same. It only takes a little squeeze, another day.

No one knows. And if no one knows then no one
will know. No eyes will see no ears will hear when
there is nothing to see and nothing to hear. And
when there is something to see and something to

hear, still no one knows, not really, sometimes even when it is happening to them. Touch, but don't look. Kiss, but don't tell. Hide, but don't seek. Kill, but don't feel. Every child is raised in this prison one way or another. I know a man who told me that when he was a boy a neighbourhood man with a metal plate in his head from the Korean War took him to a field pulled his pants down and told him *Kiss it!* He couldn't get *kiss* and *it* together. Kiss was the soft skin of his mother's cheek, the smell of his father's cigarettes. *No. Kiss it. No. Just put it in your hand and give it a little squeeze. No.* He ran to the man's car and grabbed a hammer he had seen on the floor, a hammer like the one his father used to build everything, the first time a hammer ever turned into a weapon in his hands so he knew for the first time too that sometimes things are not themselves, and as the man ran toward him calling him scumbag calling him punk calling him chicken, shouting I'm going to tell everyone you did it you little shit he swung the hammer at the man's head where he thought the metal plate might be as hot bombs exploded out of his eyes, and he swung it again and again. That was fifty years ago. No act, he said, not even a simple one is free from the olive colour of his skin, the stench of his breath, the bristle of his wiry beard. All of it now a pathway of the mind, and not mine alone, for I have told it to you. I'm sorry.

Only the imagination is real, William Carlos
Williams wrote. Only that. His red wheel barrow
and all the life unnamed that depends upon it a
tantalizing proof he left behind as the imagination
leaps to fill it up with such names. But every murder
and every act of love is the imagination leaping,
too. Every war the result of someone's wanting,
someone's good idea. Hold the light up, hold the
light up that all may see what someone wanted, my
wife wrote of Guernica. Even if you can think of an
exception it would be the imagination showing off
or tipping its hand with a triple flip in mid air. The
imagination ripens and is ripened like two lovers
naked in the world. The joy in their bodies is the
imagination swelling into form. I saw it in a couple
on the great lawn of a park in east Berlin before the
imagination brought that city back to itself. Their
lovemaking held the light up for all to see before
the wall came down, which was another light all
its own, but the prison and assassins have yet to
understand and there is much to do before the
lovers the assassins and we leave this tender world.
But do we leave? Do we enter? Was Hitler right
to have the taunt *Arbeit Macht Frei* carved over the
gateway to hell? Does being ever end?

Every act is plural. We do nothing alone. How it
feels is simply how it feels. A woman in Halifax,
or in China during the twelfth century wars that

killed her husband, writes a poem. A man on
Vancouver Island reads it. The line between them,
the continuum, is not found in the poem. After she
writes she stares through the fogged window at the
snow. "It is painful to remember spring," she writes.
"The west wind has left me / with an ancient chill."
After he reads he stares at the words but no longer
sees. We meet in the invisible world we come
from. Don't be fooled by what you see. By hearing,
smelling, tasting, touching or excitement in the
mind. Siddhartha told us this five centuries before
Pontius Pilate played his hand. Even if you think you
see or understand, the place that lives and doesn't
die, that dies and doesn't live, that doesn't live and
doesn't die, that only lives and dies, is both invisible
and found everywhere; it makes us what we are.
This is not meant as consolation. It is the world as
it is. Every breath, every death, and everything we
meet is the locus, the matrix out of which all things
come into being, but no thing is born. It is ancient
formlessness, ancient form. The slightest loss of
attention leads to etcetera.

It's time to stop the war. I beg you. Time to stop
the killing, the raping of boys and girls, women and
men, the land that keeps us alive. It's time to stop
starving and crippling the poor, the air, the forests
in Brazil. Time to stop slaughtering the animals and
frightening the imagination. It's time for the slave

ship human trade in Africa, the sweatshops in New Delhi and Shanghai, to come to an end. Time for the Arctic penetration, the narcotic spike of oil and military force, to stop. End the fear, the hatred, the manipulation. End it where we stand. I beg you. In a timeless world, it's time.

Flamenco, Blood and Song

for Lorca

Rodrigo plays. I begin to pace the floor.
A torrent of rain pours out of the mouth
of the guitar, a tower of bones,
drenched fingers, shattered spines,

hips and breasts that danced in the nightclubs
of Seville making love with the music
of their poets while the crickets of summer
called to them, lured them outside to loosen

their clothes and lie down in the shadows
together, or sing until a bloodless
dawn rose over the Guadalquivir.
Then the bombings came and the Guardia Civil.

We live in history even if it does not live in us,
even if we are blind to the hyenas
whose voices cut families in half
until the unknown graves of the disappeared
hear a proper weeping, always too late.

Green, green as the poet's eyes that loved green,
the grass that covers him.

Silver, silver as the earrings his mother
dangled over his cradle as she soothed
him with songs he would never forget.

Black, black as the uniforms,
the coffin's tight room, black
as the blood that spilled when
the executioner's bullets tore
into his throat so he would
sing no more. Black as that.

Sun drenches the towers of Córdova.
It is a new century. The assassins have moved on
to silence other songs. Do we hear them?
Will we break off from the constant noise
long enough to see their savage smiles slicing the air?

Poets cannot afford to miss this spectacle.
Women and men whose heads bend over their labours
must not forget to look up. The uniforms are not
cartoons easy to spot in a crowd. Look closely,

listen to the air that spirals and whines like a bomb,
the dust that explodes and settles with new bone.
No one is innocent in a terrible time.
Every voice given comes with a demand.

I rise long before dawn, unable to sleep again.
There is a pain in me that is not my pain alone,
a sanctuary built of other men, other mothers
who pace the night floor plotting to keep children alive.

I speak with them by staring into the dark,
by holding the ruined limbs of their young
in my imagination like talismans to keep them
from dying. It isn't enough. It isn't hardly enough.

33

The air is too warm. The rain in this northern
province falls heavily like chunks of flesh
torn from the sky. It batters the ground.
Reports from the south speak of flooding,
fires, drownings, burning, ruin.

I can't keep out of my ears the voice of a man
I saw carrying a sign:

> All wars are the same war.
> Ask the weather.

Federico, I come back to you again,
poem after poem dedicated to your sacrifice.
Night after night, even after all these years,
I sing the promise of love you gave.

Child of the unlikely light of stars.
Boy-like lover of women and men
who sang the ache and joy beneath
the rustle of their clothing, the business

is still unfinished. I have no certainty to offer.
Only the trembling of an aging man
who is either so blind, or fiercely
so in love with the world,
he has neither the time nor sense
to tremble with fear.

History

Because we live in history
I can't help but look at her.
That girl carries the face
of Serbia as if she were
carrying a flag. (My friend
Valerie told me she left Berlin
after a stranger approached
in a café and whispered,
Du hast judische Augen — You
have Jewish eyes.) Fortunately,
the girl is too young to have studied
history, and believes her blood
will always keep her warm.
Look at her! She has no question
that her face belongs solely
to her, entirely her own.

Unfinished Meditations in the Dying Room

Some things are measured in years, others in years lost.

How can you lose what you never had?

In David's case, and Anne's, half a life was whole, even if it doesn't feel so; even if it feels like everyone was robbed.

Already at thirty five she speaks of 'my dead.'

At forty one Paul writes he's 'halfway down the coast', but wants no pity for a pain he would not share. Brave poet.

At forty three Stuart shouts through the door, "Only come in if you are a poet!" It's our first meeting. I hesitate, then walk in. Phrases, one liners, entire poems scribble the walls. The only light climbs through the lowered shade. Beside his head his fierce hand has written, "If we say we'll win, we'll lose." His gentleness and smile take me by surprise from the shabby bed where he will die.

At the beginning of HIV a friend says, "I'm afraid I'm going to lose my son. He's positive." And she does. At the time I don't know what she means because positive sounds like a good thing.

Another friend says, "Your poem's not very uplifting." I think of my *sensei* whose husband died saving her, teaching me the conjugation for *agemasu:* to raise up, commonly used when one wants to serve something to another and inquires if it is something they want. A life? A cup of tea?

After a long silence, my father opens his eyes suddenly. "I'm so lucky to have people like you around me." These are the last words he will speak.

"One two three four five. What does it mean?" The last question my mother asked of me.

"Are you going to die?" my son asks. "Yes. Like everything. But not yet." Iréne was not so lucky, nor was Emiko, her five year old child.

I try to learn from the forest floor, from the rotted carcasses of ancient trees. Things grow soft, some before, some after they die. What chooses?

"I feel him around me all the time. He helps me. I know him better now that he is gone."

At the café a friend stops by. I am sitting with a

poet who moments before told me the friend's
mother had recently died. As we talk the table
fills with such parents. The three of us hold them
invisibly though we say that they hold us. Then a
coffee spills. My friend grabs a rag quickly from the
busboy's hand. I watch his great care as he cleans
up the spill.

"Go on. Aw, go on."

No beginning, no ending. Still — . Just the same — .

Ken saves his father's ashes in a beautiful urn
until years later when his mother dies. After she
is cremated we take all the ashes into the Maine
woods and dig a large hole. Then Ken stands in
the hole and pours each of their ashes into a single
mound while I chant the Heart Sutra and watch
as he mixes his parents' ashes with his hands.
Afterwards, we plant a dogwood in the hole and
cover the roots with fresh earth. Not a word
between us. As we walk away I let him go a little
ahead. Wasn't he always the two of them mixed
into one?

Some silence is healing, some is unwanted.

"Only this life, never ending," the guru said. Yes.
But what does he mean by 'this'?

Without meaning to, the dying zen master left a koan for his students when he told them, "I don't want to die." Then, just before he died, his successor asked him where they would meet. The master raised one finger and circled the air. Then he bowed into the circle.

Found

I can't find it, and when I do I can't understand
what I have found. Once again I look for a book
I've sought for weeks. It is lost in the forest of books
I call our library. Trees transformed into people's
dreams, longing, grief and losses, pages of love in
so many languages and so many fictions and forms
and always the words the words the words to say it
all forever.

As I look I suddenly recall something else I've lost.
A memory of a girl, barely a woman, I spent a night
with only once, a beautiful girl with red hair who
I knew had climbed over the fence after midnight
and gone swimming with the dolphins in their tank
at the local zoo. A girl like that is someone to spend
time with and I did. I told her I wanted to and she
said that sounded good to her so we got together
that night, had a late dinner, drank wine, and then
she showed me her translations from the poems of
Federico García Lorca. They were good and they
almost thrilled me as much as knowing that she was
a girl who would climb a fence to make that swim
though it was late autumn when she did and the
night, she said, was cold. *Frío. Yes. Mucho frío,* I
agreed.

And then she took off her orange socks and her skirt
and blouse and bra and underwear and she kneeled
down naked and unbuckled my belt and slipped off
my pants and underwear but left my socks on and
then stood up and slid my shirt over my chest and
my head and said with a grin looking down at me,
You don't look cold, you know, but I am so shall we
translate all this nakedness and cold into something
we can dance to? *Sí*, I said, to keep our joke going.
And I couldn't take my eyes off her.

I woke early and beside me on the nightstand
were the wine bottles and her black clothbound
hard-cover copy of Lorca's *Obras Completas*. We
must have read from it sometime during the night
but I didn't remember that. It's not the book I was
looking for today but it's the book I found that
brought her back to me so I could write this poem.

Take it, she said. She sounded sleepy in the way
that made me want to make love again. Take what?
I asked, hopeful. Take Lorca with you. I'm through
with him and if I need him again I'll know where
to find him. Are you sure? I'm sure. I'm sure and
I'm sleeping and you have to go now before my
daughter wakes up. I looked at her, amazed. You
have a daughter? Yes, Katie. And she's sleeping but
she won't sleep forever and you were so loving I

don't want things to get difficult or confused. Take Lorca and kiss me, go away and let me get back to sleep while I can.

So I did. And today, while looking for *19 Ways of Looking at Wang Wei,* I found my *Obras Completas* and thought of her, an Irish girl I never saw again though she filled me with longing enough to take me across Wang's ten thousand peaks to the certainty I needed when I was young that life can be surprising and good.

Beside

For the moment the sea lies easy
beside the land. Sometimes an unseen
question curls inside a fist this way,
or lovers sleep on their backs barely
touching, naked in so many ways.

It isn't only the young who know
such ease. There are times an aging
woman or man lies in bed, gazing
through the long hours, calm,
no longer troubled by the day.

Such times grow like a slow garden
out of season. Unpredictable,
they come on their own, arriving
when all seemed otherwise —
only a fool would turn away the grace
of sleepless patience and wonder.

The house is quiet now, spacious
as a mind at rest. The almost blue
night air fills with the sound of
steady breathing as the flame
of my mother's memorial candle
appears in the dark and grows still.

"Where are you?" my father called
in a dream I had just after he died.
I could hear his voice come through
from the floor above. It wasn't long
before she let go, "to be with him"
she said, faithful even past what she felt
would be the end. Now I can see them,
each holding one edge of death's handkerchief
as they're lifted by their families and friends
and dance together in the air past endings.

We are not here to prove or disprove.
Not here to instruct our senses, or correct
what we've been given as ourselves.
With luck life brings us finally past
any purpose or intention to the moment
it provides. Tonight, after a winter of great pain,
a sleepless winter where all purposes were
forcibly abandoned, now is such a time.

The image of my mother's flame disappears
and I am left only with the blueness of the air.
Beside me, my wife murmurs and turns,
her eyes following what I can't see,
though I detect the scent of fresh cut
wheat in her calm exhale.

I can make no sense of what she says,
she is wed to her own still night
as surely as we were years before,
and yet my solitude shows me
the body of night like the body of the woman
I love not only surrounds, but lies
already within like a beginningless vow
that binds us each to each, past dreaming,
past death or any ending we perceive.
To know it is finally to believe.

In Grace

for Shirley

The beans are sweet, abundant,
you pluck them from the garden
with desiring hands. Then your eyes
carry them through the meadow
to the house where you cut loose
their caps and dance them
into the waiting bowl, dreaming
the Ukrainian music of your violin.
It is a bowl you turned on the wheel
until it spun itself into a shape you
hoped would never stop turning,
a bowl glazed with a trace of blue sky
and the full lips of desire. How long
has that bowl been waiting?
How long must we wait
with desire? Love
arrives or it is delayed
or it cannot stay long enough
for the meal to reach an end.
Meanwhile the earth that flies
and will fill us at the last
fills us now with green,
with rain, with the mineral
song that weaves through eons
without ending. And you,
who long with a woman's

longing for the good of her son,
her husband, the poetry
that pours through every
moment of your living,
you sit down beside us
at the table, place
your hands quietly,
briefly in your lap.
Then you lift them,
palms together
like a tender flame
each of us holds,
and we bow.

First Snow

Yes. We used to play until the thin skins
of our gloves were soaked
and our hands ached with frost.
Then we'd find a place,
a radiator in a building where no adults
would come so we could strip off
our gloves and boots while some of us,
the brave ones, took off their pants,
and we'd warm our toes and fingers
and backsides until the frost
burned right out of them.

All the time we'd be laughing,
or sometimes crying as the heat
drew life back into our fingers,
but laughing nonetheless at the luxury
of a big snow that burst
out of the sky and how we could
scoop it up and toss it high into the air,
or throw it at each other in a ball
with shouts or challenges and shock
as some of it slipped beneath
our jacket collars and froze us
with joy all the way down.

This is how it was when I was a boy,
and this is how it is for my children
and their friends. I stand at the window
warmed by wood in the furnace
and the sight of them sledding
in the meadow below,
knowing I have lived long enough
to see nature's generosity passed on again,
while wondering how long
this laughter will last in their lives
as it has in mine, and what I can do
to help them know that hidden buds
awaken beneath every snow,
that the barest branch is nothing
but buds and blossoms waiting to be found,
and to look for this bounty,
laughing or crying, wherever they stand.

Strap

A belt when he put it on to go to work. His hands knew the tooled leather and trouser loops so well he didn't have to look as he circled his waist in the darkened room.

A strap when he threatened to use it on me and reached for the metal buckle like the butt of a gun.

A belt when he stripped it off after work and made a corral of the leather to contain the contents of his pockets on the dresser: knife, lighter, keys, handkerchief, change.

A strap when he said the word "strap" and I could hear in the deep tone of his voice the threat of leather slapping skin.

A belt when I would secretly stand in his dimly lit closet and slide the smooth, tanned animal hide through my fingers.

A strap when he told how his mother had used a cat o' nine-tails on him. "It's like a whip," he said, when I asked if it was really made of cat's tails; imagining them soft, wanting them to be soft, wanting, if I was to be hit, to be hit by something soft. He said he kept it on the top shelf of his closet, too high for me to see.

Strap when I imagined the cat o' nine-tails coiled there waiting.

Strap when I looked for it and couldn't find it.

Strap when he opened the closet door and found me standing on his tool box, looking. Strap when I lied and said I wanted to wear one of his hats on the top shelf and came out with a large soft, felt one. Strap as he smiled when I put on his hat and it slipped down over my eyes. Sliced across his brown face, his white teeth made a strap of a smile.

Belt when he used it to hold up his pants.

Strap when he pulled down mine.

For years whenever I got my hands on a belt I used to double it back on itself so that the tip and buckle ends would meet and the belt would become a leather circle. Then, holding the ends of the belt tightly in my two small fists, I would bring my hands slightly together in front of my chest to allow the middle of the belt to fall slack like a sleeping mouth, and when it was time, when the soft, unsuspecting leather lips of the belt grew so limp that they opened completely, I'd snap it all together and make a sharp crack like the sound of a pistol going off. In this way I turned the soft leather of a belt into the sound of the dreaded strap. In this way I played when I was alone. In this way I survived the repetition of that sound, again and again and again.

The Swing

The swing hangs
from a high branch
above a broken ladder

it floats there
a promise
moved by a slight wind

the child cannot see,
it taunts him
teaches him

until his arms ache
to wrap themselves
around the braided ropes

and his body longs
to feel itself settled
on the empty plank

between them.
Finally, he does,
he climbs the rungs

of the broken ladder
until he holds the ropes
and presses his small

full weight
onto the seat
of his beloved swing.

Then he pulls himself
from the shadow behind
skyward toward the light

kicking the ladder down.
Back and forth he swings
and rocks and shouts

not knowing
his kicks and bellowing
begin the man

he will become
long after the empty swing
taunts another child

and another
to reach, to climb
or to fall.

The Moment

My little boy in big black boots
is down in the meadow raking,
already some of the man he will be.
I watch for a while then turn away
before he can see me. The moment
is his and will be raked into memory
as were times when I rode my bicycle
or stood at the edge of a lake and cried.

It has that quietude, intensity.

He doesn't look up even when the nearby
robins cry out against invading crows.
I am glad. He has found a way to be alone
with the world before him, and when
he does look up, his face will glow
with what he has made and known.

A Game of Miracles

1.

My son and I play a game
naming everything we see
in fifteen seconds of opening
our eyes as we sit under
our special tree overlooking
the ocean. We fail and try again.
I tell him they say the Buddha
sat under a tree for seven days
and nights until he finally saw
the morning star. No one ever
succeeds at our game but we
can't help noticing this, too.

2.

Dogen wrote there are three
million miracles every morning,
and eight hundred thousand
in the afternoon. When Kaz
told me this I thought maybe
miracles got tired from being
awake and busy so early every
day so they took a sort of siesta
like I've heard they do in Spain
until the evening fireworks begin.

3.

I don't like to kill flies
because they have eyesight
and some people would give
everything to trade places
with a fly. I don't say
those who do kill flies
are bad, especially black flies
in early summer in Maine,
but I feel bad when I see it
just the same. I remember
Issa, a poet who moved deep
into the mountains after
his wife and children
were killed. One day,
just before walking
out of his hut to gather
wood, he wrote,
I'm leaving.
You can make love now,
my flies.

4.

Because the world is round
I am here. If it was flattened
out I might still be here,
but it is as it is and that

shouldn't be ignored,
don't you think?

5.

I am up early writing
not because I can't sleep,
but because I can be

1) up
2) early
3) writing

I once heard a woman
say there is room for
everything, that's why
it's here. I thought,
even me.

6.

A few days after
my mother died
my wife came upstairs
when she heard me yell,
Mom, where are you?
She was just a little
concerned and said,
have you forgotten

your mother died?
No, I said.
But what's that got
to do with it?
I want her.

7.

I get up from writing
this poem and look
towards the lake:
a woman is fishing
from a red canoe.

8.

In Buddhism they say
each thing is as it is
because all things
are as they are:
this is like this
because that is like that.
This is not like this
because that is not like that.
Modern people are very smart,
but often they're also unhappy.
www. they write, but do they
know what it means?

9.

One day my teacher
held up a fishing net.
Because this has holes,
he said, it's a net.
It's important to know
what things are. This
net can hold many fish,
but the holes come with it.

The Question

for Iréne Pijoan,
1953-2004

Last night I dreamed of you again
in your studio as usual.
The dusk of your face,
the framing fall of your hair,
a study in dark and light.
I remember how little you would say
about your paintings, though often
you'd pace with the fevered
question of your art and fill the room
with joy after they were done.

"It's a way I have to meet my father,"
you'd say, "since he died when I was three."
Mother of five year old Emiko who played
in the other room while you showed me the place
where your nipple was removed and laughed
that now you'd have to sew a flower on,
I wish you could tell me:
Was it said, did your passion
press itself deep enough into paint and canvas
before cancer drained the colour from your brush?

A Poet

Every time he writes of the ocean
he writes of breath. A woman,
a man, night, stars, longing,
for him it's the breath of these
by the sea he wants for his poem.
Maybe because he's Italian or once
was in love or maybe because he's
growing old and beginning to count
his breaths to the last he doesn't mind
finding it again and again. Who can say?
I read him patiently, willing to wait
for the alfalfa to grow in a field
where the roughened stones have been
smoothed, or for the love he remembers
to quietly fold its hands and close its eyes.
Then, I tell him, you will not need to have
so much breathing or make anything be
the way you want it to be. He smiles
when he hears this, and goes on
one year and poem after another,
filling his universe with oxygen,
the only way he's found to stay alive.

Ancestors at the Sizzling Szechuan Palace

The restaurant is crowded, noisy,
steam clouds flee the kitchen heat
while outside the traffic river honks
through the chair-propped door.
I bury myself in a cup of coarse tea,
a bowl of plain rice, but when I look up
it all comes clear —
this is the heaven realm of bodhisattvas.
One stands squeezed between chairs
in the aisle and nurses her newborn
beside the flashing Tsing Tao sign,
another feeds her daughter fried string beans
with chop sticks one by one. Grandfather
with thick ears is yelling to his wife who leans
closer, smiling, nodding Yes! Yes! deaf to
everything he and everyone else has to say,
boys with large grins tussle over the last spare rib,
shiny haired girls kick each other under the table
with their spanking new leather shoes.
Wake up! Wake up! they all say.
Keep doing the best you can!
And suddenly a homeless man with a bright
watermelon patch of skin over half his face
and not a tooth in his mouth rushes in
and scurries from table to table like a whirlwind
that pats the children on their heads and laughs

with his arms around the old folks like friends
at a wedding before chasing himself out the door
and leaving behind a breeze that blows all the way
from the Yangtse at Liang right through this palace
of human love and cools us with a joy rarely seen.
Pretty soon we settle into the chattering hum again
as Grandmother continues to nod and smile,
but there is a quiet happiness at each table
that wasn't here before, and beneath the hum
the sound of Bodhidharma's straw sandals
can be heard as he steps from his floating leaf
onto fertile Chinese soil.

Beginning

Just after dawn
five young deer gather
beside the garden gate
until a sound I can't hear
makes their hooves disappear
into mist coming off the lake.
Quietly, I move a little further
down the path to stand
where they have been.
Doe prints on spring moss
begin the morning —
I wonder about the day.

Who Else Then?

For Galway Kinnell

Rains driven from the north
pound the metal roof like roans in fright
threatening to break right through.
It puts me in the mood for Irish
questions that quip at an angle
and smile: How did a man like you
get a name like a city, Galway,
for you must know by now
it has that sort of ring?

Or maybe I mistake things as I often do
and you possess not a city's name
but the name of a country, or a world.
And how as a man with such a name did you
learn to love things of the world so much?
Was the heft of your name a factor?
Did you learn to see because you had to
twice what an ordinary man might see,
and hear and feel and know and name doubly?
Is one of the Druidic meanings of Galway
he who twices everything? It could be.

I love your blackberry thumbs, poet,
your bear grips, the savour
each syllable becomes as it rolls
down the fully throated streets of Galway

late into the night, and I love your loving it
as much or more than I, for let's be poets,
Galway, and always tell everything.

Suddenly I realize the rain has completely disappeared
and the room where I write echoes the late night solitude
that fills these hours like the sound of monastery bells.
Galway has written his whole life long, but I cannot
find a shred of poem in any thought that passes
ghostlike for thinking. Was I wrong from the start
to call a man a city when really he was the rain?
It could be so. Or has he carried the rain away
in secret and left me to seek it out in the words
I find for this poem or the next? Galway,
you're a shifty fellow to do a thing like that.
I'm half inclined to write a poem
about Kinnell, just to get even.

Now the dark you can't see, the dark
behind the latest part of evening comes in
bringing with it a gentle rain. I can feel you, poet,
I can hear the laughing look you gave your boy
as you tucked him in again so many years ago.

Go, now. Go, city of a man
with the sure restraint of country manners.
Nothing calls you as much as love,
and she is yours to have as you return
the gifts that she has given.

I will remain, content with the deep in darkness
of the night, the soft finger taps of rain calming
the roof bound horses, stroking their steaming necks
and manes that shiver and scatter crystals into the air,
until the next time we meet, perhaps beside
a frozen river, the still world of waist high snow,
the cedars across the meadow ablaze with all we love.

In The Dark

for R.C.

Not yet dawn, they don't see me
as they arrive with poles and buckets,
fishing nets filling their hands.

I only just make out the two of them,
slim shadows beneath a new moon
on this beach north of Michoacán.

They step quickly on wet sand,
pile their load into the boat
without a word or sound

as they do every day, first
one then the other who holds
a pole between his teeth

and unhitches the worn
rope from its holding stone.
Then they push their small

skiff toward the surf and I lose
sight completely as they enter
the blinding sound of waves.

It hurts to be so far from where
you died, Bob, though the living
are always a distance from the dead.

Three nights since and I still can't find
anyone who knows where to reach
Penelope to say the little I can. Love,

certainly grief. The painful truth
of words that fail. I hate
that you died needing a way

to breathe. A cruel trick though
you'd deny any intention
and say, "We live as we live,

one foot following etc. until
we don't etc." A poem's
prosodic measure, nothing more.

And you'd be right. Everything does
happen, given time. Just before
your 75th I sent a note but was off

by a month and you wrote quickly,
"Not yet, ha ha, old friend." The joy
of beating it back even thirty days

and living to say so with your knowing
laugh, an offering as always —
you are that friend.

Now the light begins to lift itself
into the sky. Not the light you
railed against in metaphor,

pointing to a dim bulb beneath
a bar shade, saying, "Is that
the light you mean?"

No. But a gentler seeing is made
by its gradual rise and the waves
the young fishers are out among

grow calm enough to help them
gain their morning catch
while softening the many deaths

of recent years and forgiving
the darkest fear I hold of the sea.
Hard to live each day the next

in the shadow of all that's lost,
hard not to, truth to tell.
I had wanted to let you know

before my mother died, gone
by then to all intents of the mind,
I uncurled her paralytic hand

and counted for her each finger in turn.
"One two three four five.
Say it, mother, if you can."

But she looked away as so often
she did near the end and made
no sound. Next day as I entered

the room she looked to where I stood,
her youngest so recently unknown.
"One," she said, and slightly lifted her hand.

"One two three four five."
Suddenly I recalled she was the one
who taught me counting and all the words

in turn. Then she rested her eyes
on my face and asked the last thing
I would hear her say:

"What does it mean?"
And I found myself in the dark
as now I am again,

watching the light rise higher
into the Mexican sky with just enough
glimmer to begin to see.

A Dream of Candour

I always admired them,
the horses that pulled heavy wagons
down the avenue when I was a child,
the donkeys hoofing up the village hills
on marble steps, the birds dodging traffic,
the squirrels and occasional city rat,
and especially the most ordinary
cat or dog walking slowly down
the centre of the street, naked,
unconcerned as sunlight
in the middle of an afternoon.

Conjugation

to concur
to agree

to occur
to happen

to agree
to happen

to happen
to agree

to a degree
it happens

The Screen Door Slams

for Bob Creeley

Dear friend, gone
now inside where
you never truly
left. Not only
*'the figure of
outward'*,
the inward
presence grows
strong. Thirty eight
years don't
flash by,
but today
they come
as one. Love's
gift, I suppose,
its generosity
and demand.
Onward! seems
more lonely
now — but I
will, to honor
what's made,
and will be,
somehow.

Entrance to the
Stone Hill Pub

I see them coming from where I sit
in the garden, the gentle curve
of a stone stacked wall behind me,
the maple towering above the flowering
apple, and all around the signs of an early
and plentiful spring. Up the hill and slowly
they come, then, walking one by one in
the disinterested confines of their family.
The son appears first, a young man of twenty,
too thin in the cheek. The daughter is not,
seemingly born within a year of the boy
she carries her weight awkwardly and walks
closely behind. Then the mother arrives,
detached from them all. Her movements are
anxious, her eyes dart between the stonework,
her daughter, and the trees. The father lags behind,
a small man who worries the knuckle of one hand
with the thumb of the other, his mind pressed darkly
into his eyes. If something is wrong here, I wouldn't
know how to say it, or what it is, but a sudden wind
rises in the forest behind them as they approach
howling like a ghost in anguish through the trees.

Even So

Down the road a man builds a stone wall. Each day he sizes the stones, finding the balance, mixes his concrete with a trowel, and one or two new stones appear beside the others. My wife and I laugh to see how slowly he builds the wall, but every day we return to see how it grows. Once, while he was working, I heard him tell a neighbour, "One skin clothes us all." I went home and sat by myself for hours. When my wife came I told her what he said. Then we stood side by side cutting vegetables. The carrot pieces fell from the blade until they made a small pile on the cutting board. Then the green onions did the same. And the peppers, cucumbers, beans, asparagus, tomatoes, broccoli, red leaf lettuce, spinach, cheeses, and finally, after throwing it all into a wooden bowl, I placed a handful of sunflower seeds at the centre in a small mound. All this time we did not speak of the man down the road, or his stone wall, or what I heard him tell the neighbour. Sometime before he finished the wall, my wife moved away to live in another city. Even so, I've lived this man's way ever since we made that salad, and the hunger's not as bad as it was before.

Shoes

The boys found the old woman
before anyone else. In a moment
they knew she was dead. While
the youngest checked her breathing
one of the older boys went to the foot
of the bed, untied her laces, then tied them
together in a knot. He was never able to tell
himself why. Then they fled to the narrow alleys
where they played until one by one manhood
or war took most of them away.

The boy who tied her shoes together
never thought of her again. He lived
a long life in the village and gathered children
and grandchildren and great grandchildren
like so many olives in the groves he picked.
One day he didn't show up to sit on the bench
with the others who leaned on their canes
during the hour of great light before evening.
They sent some boys to his stone house
to convince him to come to the plaza like always.
The boys came back empty-handed. The old man
refused to leave his bed. "The old woman is coming,"
he told them. "I can hear her old shoes walking."
He lifted his hand and they saw the long nail tremble.

Where You Find It

I had seen the white bird
several times, once
too high to say for sure,
another time in Spain
among the shattered
towers ruined by war.
Now she came again
as I sat with my toes
buried in light sand
beside the sea. She
was courageous
and drew near
incrementally,
each hop
scattering sand
from her delicate
feet. So close,
I thought, and gently
reached out my hand.
Gone. Back into the air.
I lowered my eyes.
Beside me was a shell
I hadn't seen before.
I picked it up and looked
at both sides with my fingers.
White.
White as feathers, as bone.

A Dream of Heaven

A few minutes ago my wife went out
to buy groceries and left me with the
monitor so I can hear the baby if he
wakes up alone in his room. He rasps
with a terrible cold. I go into my studio,
set the monitor beside me on the table,
and begin to read the day's work. After
only a minute I realize I am breathing
hard, as if I had just run out to get some
firewood at the beginning of a storm. But
it is my son's breathing coming through
the monitor that has entered my body
and become my own. I lift the white
plastic voice box of my son and hold it
to my ear. In, out. In, out. In, out. And
I wonder, almost pleading, let me hear it
just like this, after I die.

At the Lake

First the red wing blackbird
skims the surface, the male
doing a little reconnaissance
before settling
just above the nettle.
Then the ducks sweep in
to swim among the weeds
twenty feet from shore.
Now the geese appear
without warning
from a break in the alder.
They land heavily
with a large splash
just past their log. At last
the blue heron arrives,
circling, commanding,
until everyone disappears.
He swims to the tallest reeds
and suddenly turns shy,
insinuating himself like a shadow
into the patch of yellow iris.
Now it's my turn.
I pour myself quietly
in from an angle
I hope the heron
doesn't see. He does.
His great prehistoric wings

lift him from his hidden place
into the sky. I watch as he goes.
Good bye, heron. I
know I'll see you tomorrow.
These meetings are our summer
romance, our fleeting love.

For The Old Man

What grows cold
is love's body
pulling in, seeking
in contraction
what expansion
had given years before:
shelter, touch,
a place or person
belonged to,
or the chance
to be called that name
for a time. I can't
really fault the design
as life comes to an end
that it must be so,
having seen it over
and over in the lives of
good women, good men.

The mind wanders,
the body droops,
makes a sound
declining more
of almost everything,
not out of distaste
but as a modesty,
a recognized

self condition,
the integrity
to sit awhile
where one can
amidst all that rushes by,
and then slowly,
seeming almost
not to move,
to move on.

First Red

1.

It is a nightly parade
in black and white.

Up and down
they walk,

the young and old
alike on this

southern island's
southmost town.

The young men
in clusters,

the girls
by twos,

and the old couples
beside each other

as they have
and their ancestors

forever, all of them
tipping hats,

nodding heads
or shrugging,

a gesture they don't
know they do.

Among them
a girl walks

at sunset
in red shoes,

her mother's.
She steps

through shadows
on the cobbled square,

red shoes, red
as if she was the tallest

stalk, the most beautiful amaryllis,
red shoes, red shoes,

is all the sound
she hears.

2.

The scene a single
thread an old man

still holds, his memory
a stamen

thrusting its powdered
head red against

white petals
as he leans on

a broken window ledge
in summer.

Who could know the girl
had been his fancy,

an image
carried in his boyish mind

as he walked
in red shoes,

his full joy
turned to shame

by a father's slap,
the redness

of cheek and jaw
still ripe,

the sound still heard
all these years?

3.

What a shape it makes,
a hand

on flesh
stopping time,

the welt
marking

the day
the hour

of red shoes
desire

and shame.
Never

never, never
never the same,

eyes look down
from a blank

window
onto stones,

a cobbled
fear

on the public
square.

Fundamental

Sitting quietly with Dogen's
Actualizing the Fundamental Point
I hear rain begin to splatter
against the eaves. Even
though I know *as it is*
this should be enough,
I am still young in the Way—
I light the white candle beside me,
to warm the storm from inside.

Hope

In the small village
with white houses
and the sea painting
echoes on shutters
and domes

the young girl's
eyes are magenta
with longing. She
walks on narrow
marble paths
made for donkeys
as if for queens

and takes the sway
from olive groves
into her slim hips
when no one is looking

with their olive eyes.
What she sees
sharp as a thorn
is the stitch
the horizon makes

between this world
and the next. Her

god a lover
who comes like mist
in the morning
and leaves a promise
in the sunlight
at noon.

"Foolish
foolish girl,"
they say at night
when she comes home,
"always looking
into nowhere."
But she knows them,
knows for them the silver
moon is dead, a mere
currency they pass
from face to face.

Village Song

"Life is simple. Life is simple.
All the girls are dancing."

In the grove not far off
the sea rocks and the small
abandoned church
white in the southern
slant of the sun,
the young man peels
a tangerine
as if undressing
dawn and the girl
who would dance with him
no more. Slowly
he fingers the supple
skin and lifts one
crescent at a time,
eating then tasting
his loss again
and again.

Drowned girl of the groves,
black haired iridescence
whose eyes shone
like the church dome
blessed by the colour
of sky meeting sea,
a grey snake
filled and took you
down to the home your

poets only sang about,
meaning their god,
not the sweet ache
of yearning, never
again to be found.

Barefoot girl who laughed
and danced with a kelp
necklace draped to your
naked waist, the music
of far off death
came to your village,
close enough
to touch you
who alone
dove into the waters.

With his back
beginning to dissolve
like early mist
into the rough bark
of the olive tree,
the young man sinks
his nail into the soft
skin, then peels
another small fruit
as if he could
undress death,
take it back
to nothing
beside the sea.

In Provence

At the very edge
death begins to fold the page,

the farmer puts the paper down
with its wars and ads

and too bright smiles.
The sun makes a breeze

of green above him
in the over arching pear tree,

and a line from Rilke
learned as a child

marches before his eyes
like a line of ants.

Beauty, beauty, he says,
and the poet agreed,

looking past all the years
and distances from then

to here, where a man
would need him,

his words the final
benediction of all

the grey, the yellow,
the brown, the green

the rains and drought
the fat fruit, the bursting

clouds and finally her,
the maker never unmade

by sickle thin harvests
or the need for more

patience than anyone could bear.
Beauty, beauty,

he says and the poet
in another country

wrote the words just as he
would need them,

a blessing at the end
of his time.

Paper

for S. at Pefki

She came barefoot through the grove
below their mountain town. A dancer,
she always walked slowly, her soles
pressing the moist grass and soft earth
until she could feel the pain of small rocks
pushing against them from the ground.
Many lovers, she smiled, and did not run past.

Above her the southern sky began to swirl,
blue turning white. A hot wind blowing north
from the African coast. Summer crows bit through
the air with their hunger and lighted on the trees
around. She began to skip on a steep descent,
the fruit she held crackling moisture against her palm.

The crows left off watching the bright crown of her
hair as it alternately hid and emerged beneath them.
They leapt from the trees with a cry and started
flight heavily. She could feel the powerful wings
lift their bodies as they gained the air, their sound
the cutting whisper of a saw. She thought they looked
like an old alphabet receding into the paper of the sky.

As she approached a narrow part of the trail,
stones of a ruined house could be seen
covered by brush in the ravine where it stood.
The town had fewer children since many families
had moved to the mainland and those who remained

did not play in the ruins as they had when she was a child.
She felt that childhood move through her as she passed.

When she came into a clearing between two of the oldest
trees in the grove she looked behind for the first time.
Far above, the whitewashed houses with their tiled
roofs seemed to hang unreal almost unseen in the air.
And again, pressed flat against the white sky they
were no more than an image fading back into paper.

She turned to descend the last part of the trail
before she would leave the grove and climb
down the jagged rocks on her way to the cove.
From where she stood she could hear the deep
sound of the waters echo in the caves below.
On her way to them she knew she would have to
balance on flat surfaces when she could.

She sighed loudly as if to answer the echo and made
a circle of both arms joined at the hands, the nest
of her fingers holding the fruit just below her waist.
Her secret child had not yet begun, but she knew
he would come to her and already she could feel him.

Soon, she told him. Soon my love. She swayed
and almost sang out: Skin, eyelids thin as paper,
fingernails, buds of arms, shoulders, elbows, toes,
ears to hear this sea, the music of your father's
instrument, his deep voice as we dance,
circle and dance among the trees, among
all that has been given, waiting for us now.

The Confession

for Shug

A beautiful iris by my side
helps me tell you this.
And cold rain. There
is no confession to look for,
our bodies remain the heart's
geometry, a geomancy that divines
among fields of stone a place
of tender earth where we've lain
again and again, toes
digging into the loose dirt,
shouts crying back to the birds
wild for what they might find
growing from the twisting root
we became. That field,
and the one with snow or
the one where the river
poured its sound over us
as you bent to the fallen
tree, my hands gripping
you from behind. So many
places love's been found
beside the quiet certainty
death's let in, the clarity
it's given to spur us on.

The Goatherd At Home

for Caliope and Yanni

"Passion's light,"
she winked,
"grows soft
as skin does,
softer still,
not more dim

becomes
a secret
more dear
than what
it remembers
from before.

I prefer
the lover
I am
now," she laughed,
"though maybe
he's not
so sure. But
I tell
you, it is better
at any age
when the thought
of death
has made
the two of you
a menage."